Jesus
the Healer

A Guided Discove ... *individuals*

LaVonne Neff

LOYOLAPRESS.
CHICAGO

LOYOLAPRESS.

3441 N. ASHLAND AVENUE
CHICAGO, ILLINOIS 60657
(800) 621-1008
WWW.LOYOLABOOKS.ORG

Nihil Obstat
Reverend John G. Lodge, S.S.L., S.T.D.
Censor Deputatus
November 7, 2004

Imprimatur
Most Reverend Raymond E. Goedert, M.A., S.T.L., J.C.L.
Vicar General
Archdiocese of Chicago
November 10, 2004

The *Nihil Obstat* and *Imprimatur* are official declarations that a book is free of doctrinal and moral error. No implication is contained therein that those who have granted the *Nihil Obstat* and *Imprimatur* agree with the content, opinions, or statements expressed. Nor do they assume any legal responsibility associated with publication.

Interior design by Kay Hartmann/Communique Design
Illustration by Anni Betts

ISBN 0-8294-2066-5

Printed in the United States of America
05 06 07 08 09 10 Bang 10 9 8 7 6 5 4 3 2 1

Contents

How to Use This Guide

You might compare the Bible to a national park. The park is so large that you could spend months, even years, getting to know it. But a brief visit, if carefully planned, can be enjoyable and worthwhile. In a few hours you can drive through the park and pull over at a handful of sites. At each stop you can get out of the car, take a short trail through the woods, listen to the wind blowing through the trees, get a feel for the place.

In this booklet, we will read stories from the four Gospels—Matthew, Mark, Luke, and John—about Jesus the healer. Because the excerpts are short, we will be able to take a leisurely walk through them, thinking carefully about what we are reading and what it means for our lives today.

This guide provides everything you need to explore Jesus' healing stories in six discussions—or to do a six-part exploration on your own. The introduction on page 6 will prepare you to get the most out of your reading. The weekly sections provide explanations that will help illuminate the meanings of the readings for your life. Equally important, each section supplies questions that will launch your group into fruitful discussion, helping you to both investigate the healing stories for yourself and learn from one another. If you're using the booklet by yourself, the questions will spur your personal reflection.

Each discussion is meant to be a *guided discovery.*

Guided. None of us is equipped to read the Bible without help. We read the Bible *for* ourselves but not *by* ourselves. Scripture was written to be understood and applied in the community of faith. So each week "A Guide to the Reading," drawing on the work of both modern biblical scholars and Christian writers of the past, supplies background and explanations. The guide will help you grasp the meanings of the healing stories. Think of it as a friendly park ranger who points out noteworthy details and explains what you're looking at so you can appreciate things for yourself.

Discovery. The purpose is for *you* to interact with the stories about Jesus' healings. "Questions for Careful Reading" is a tool to help you dig into the text and examine it carefully. "Questions for Application" will help you consider what these words mean for your life here and now. Each week concludes with an "Approach to Prayer" section that helps you respond to God's word. Supplementary "A Living Tradition" and "Saints in the Making" sections offer the thoughts and experiences of Christians past and present. By showing what Jesus' healings have meant to others, these sections will help you consider what they mean for you.

How long are the discussion sessions? We've assumed you will have about an hour and a half when you get together. If you have less time, you'll find that most of the elements can be shortened somewhat.

Is homework necessary? You will get the most out of your discussions if you read the weekly material and prepare your answers to the questions in advance of each meeting. If participants are not able to prepare, have someone read the "Guide to the Reading" sections aloud to the group at the points where they appear.

What about leadership? If you happen to have a world-class biblical scholar in your group, by all means ask him or her to lead the discussions. In the absence of any professional Scripture scholars, or even accomplished amateur biblical scholars, you can still have a first-class Bible discussion. Choose two or three people to take turns as facilitators, and have everyone read "Suggestions for Bible Discussion Groups" (page 76) before beginning.

Does everyone need a guide? a Bible? Everyone in the group will need his or her own copy of this booklet. It contains all the stories discussed in the weekly sessions, so a Bible is not absolutely necessary—but each participant will find it useful to have one. Some of the questions and commentary suggest reading passages of Scripture that are not included in this booklet. You should have at least one Bible on hand for your discussions (see page 80 for recommendations).

How do we get started? Before you begin, take a look at the suggestions for Bible discussion groups (page 76) or individuals (page 79).

Good News Made Visible

S omebody you know needs to be healed.

Imagine for a moment that you've been thinking about this person. You've been wondering if he's going to survive his illness or injuries, or you've been worrying about the quality of care she's getting in her nursing home, or you've been racking your brain for ways to pay for a pile of new prescriptions, or maybe you're so tired you're just wishing it would all end.

You flip on the TV and suddenly, sandwiched between slick commercials for expensive pharmaceuticals, you see a young man trying to move through a noisy crowd. A reporter's voice cuts through the din. "By all accounts he is trying to avoid publicity," she says, "but with a track record like his, the word is going to get out. They say that when he walks through a village, everyone is healed. People are swarming from miles around, bringing babes in arms, leading blind people by the hand, carrying people on their backs or on stretchers . . ."

How do you react?

❑ I wish TV news shows would stop using sensationalism to raise their ratings.

❑ Is this for real? Are the witnesses believable? Is someone investigating what's going on?

❑ This is spooky. Is it safe? What does it mean?

❑ Where is this guy? I want to go see him.

Two thousand years ago, people living near the eastern shores of the Mediterranean were hearing amazing stories about a young wonder-worker from Nazareth. Jesus, said to be the carpenter Joseph's son, was restoring sight to the blind and hearing to the deaf, making the crippled walk, straightening deformed limbs, banishing leprosy and fevers, and even casting out demons and raising the dead.

This was big news, and it provoked huge questions—the same questions we would ask today if the same stories were circulating. During the next six weeks we're going to look at several stories about Jesus the healer in hopes of learning more about Jesus, about healing, and about how Jesus is still at work in the world.

Different ways of reading the stories. Our source material comes mainly from the Gospels, the first four books of the New Testament: Matthew, Mark, Luke, and John. They are not biographies of Jesus or histories of first-century Judaism but books of faith. "We believe in Jesus," they all say in one way or another, "and this is why." We will also read some poems from the Old Testament book of Isaiah; the Guide to the Reading in Week 1 explains why.

People respond to the healing stories in the Gospels quite differently. Some think the stories are literally true down to the tiniest detail. If you had been in Jerusalem with your camcorder and filmed Jesus healing the man born blind (Week 6), such people believe, not only would you have captured the moment of transition from blindness to seeing, you would also have recorded the exact conversations between Jesus, the blind man, the Pharisees, and the blind man's parents that the Gospel of John describes. People who take the Bible this literally can have a great time in a discussion group as long as they don't get bogged down in details or in arguments with people who understand the stories somewhat differently.

Others dismiss these stories out of hand. Thomas Jefferson, a rationalist to the core, made a copy of the New Testament with everything miraculous edited right out of it. He was willing to believe the Bible's moral philosophy but not its supernatural elements. Those, he thought, belonged to an outdated, superstitious way of thinking. Such intense rationalism went out of date in the twentieth century as physicists and mathematicians discovered that the laws of nature are a lot more flexible than Enlightenment scientists had suspected, but a lot of people are still eager to explain away anything that appears miraculous. If confirmed rationalists and staunch literalists are in the same discussion group, things can get exciting!

Quite a few people nowadays take yet another path. People who understand miraculous stories literally are premodern (in other words, naive), they say, while people who discount them altogether are modern (that is, mechanistic) in their thinking.

Today it's more popular to be postmodern: to accept the stories as metaphors or symbols, interact with them, and look for their significance in our own lives. This postmodern approach has a lot of advantages for a discussion group. It allows everyone to delve into the stories without getting hung up on questions of what actually happened. It positively encourages group interaction, personal application, and a search for meaning. But it can cause problems if it leads people to believe that everything is relative and all truth is up for grabs.

This guide is going to take still another approach. (You don't have to agree with its approach in order to participate, but it's only fair to let you know what to expect.) With the rationalists we appreciate clear thinking and sound scholarship, especially on a topic like healing, where desperation can make anyone gullible. With the literalists we believe there is good reason to believe Jesus actually did heal a lot of people, even though we also accept the judgment of Scripture scholars who leave room to debate the stories' details. And with the postmodernists, we believe the healing stories in the Gospels have something important to say to our lives today.

Why it's okay to believe the miracles happened.
There is no way to prove that Jesus did or did not heal anybody two thousand years ago. No journalists wrote extensive reports on his actions. No medical personnel wrote down and archived case notes of the cures. But there are still reasons to believe that when Jesus showed up, people were healed.

We may not personally remember World War II, but we have personal knowledge of it from our parents, our grandparents, our teachers. If we read an interpretation of World War II that completely contradicts what we know to be true—such as, for example, one that denies the Holocaust—we strongly object. Similarly, when the Gospels began to circulate some thirty to forty years after the Crucifixion, people still had personal knowledge of Jesus, and they did not object to the fact that miracles play a huge role in all four of them. Over 30 percent of Mark, probably the first Gospel to be written, has to do with Jesus' miracles. Theologian

René Latourelle, S.J., says that "the Gospel of Mark without the miracles would be like Shakespeare's *Hamlet* without the prince." Christians accepted the Gospels because they already knew the stories and believed them to be true.

Non-Christians also believed Jesus was a wonder-worker. A Jewish source, the Babylonian Talmud, refers to Jesus' "apostasy" and "sorcery," no doubt a negative spin on what Christians called teaching and miracle working. Father John P. Meier, professor of New Testament at Notre Dame University, says this about another contemporary account:

Josephus, a first-century Jewish historian hailing from Palestine, spends only a few words on Jesus' public ministry, but prominent in his thumbnail sketch is the claim that Jesus was "a doer of startling deeds." . . . Along with Jesus' being a wise man and a teacher who attracted a large following, miracle-working is all that Josephus mentions about the public ministry before he abruptly tells us that Jesus was accused by Jewish leaders to Pilate, who condemned him to be crucified. Thus Josephus, as well as the Gospels, leaves us with the impression that Jesus' *reputation* for working miracles played no little part in his ability to attract both the favor of the crowds and the not-so-favorable attention of the authorities.

Jesus' miracles, in short, were a matter of public record. Many people did not appreciate Jesus, and some even thought he was evil, but nobody in the first century suggested that he did not actually perform miracles. In fact, miracles had a lot to do with his celebrity. "To be blunt," Meier concludes, "without miracles, one wonders how much popularity this particular Jewish preacher and teacher would have enjoyed."

The meaning of miracles. But what exactly is a miracle? Theologians who have wrestled with this question have come up with several distinguishing characteristics, all of which must be present in order for an event to be called a miracle.

A miracle is an event that transcends the laws of nature. It is not a miracle to recover from a high fever; people do that all the time. It may be a miracle, however, to recover instantly when someone walks into your bedroom and tells the fever to leave.

A miracle is something God does, not something we do. It is not a miracle to try to cure the sick by saying exactly the right words or by mixing up potions by the light of the full moon. That is magic, not miracle. It may be a miracle, however, if a person recovers when we ask God to heal him or her.

A miracle tells us something about God. It is not just an extraordinary event; it is an event with a meaning. The Church has investigated thousands of claims of miraculous healing. Many of them have been found to have no scientific explanations, but unless they have clear spiritual significance, the Church does not recognize them as miracles. A marvel without a meaning is as lifeless as a body without a soul.

What, then, do Jesus' miracles say about God? We will see in Week 1 that Jesus came to announce the good news of God's kingdom, or reign. When God reigns, the way of the world is turned upside down. As Mary sang in the Magnificat, God "has brought down the powerful from their thrones, and lifted up the lowly; he has filled the hungry with good things, and sent the rich away empty" (Luke 1:52–53). In God's kingdom, people are just, loving, and healthy. With Jesus among us, miracles of healing and new life can't help bursting out all over. Miracles, one theologian says, are "the good news itself made visible."

We will be looking at six things Jesus' healing miracles say about the kingdom of God:

1. Where Jesus is, the kingdom is present.
2. In the kingdom, the earth is restored to its original goodness and wholeness.
3. God cares for the marginalized, the weak, and even the dead.
4. God cares for not only the people of God but the entire world.
5. God cares for those who are so completely beyond hope that they can't even ask for help.
6. When we recognize that God reigns, our eyes are opened, and we see everything differently.

God's kingdom has come, and it is for everybody.

The most important question. Meanwhile, of course, we continue to live in a highly imperfect world. When theologians write about the reign of God, they often use the words *already* and *not yet:* The kingdom was already visible in Jesus Christ and continues with us through his Spirit, but it is not yet complete. We are still waiting for paradise to be restored. So in the interim, what do we make of miracles?

Theologian Hans Küng writes:

Miracles alone prove nothing. Even for Jesus' contemporaries they were ambiguous. Each one's attitude to Jesus . . . decided whether one and the same deed was the effect of God's power or a diabolic snare. This attitude decided whether [a person who saw a miracle] would allow himself to be convinced or would evade the challenge, whether he worshiped or cursed. . . . The crucial question for *Christian* faith is the question about this Christ himself: what think you of him?

We will look at miracles that happened two thousand years ago and at miracles that are happening today. We will see some saints healing people miraculously and other saints healing them through medical care. We will consider the sacrament of Anointing the Sick, and we will ask why some people are not healed. In this book there are many questions designed to stimulate thinking and evoke discussion. To understand Jesus the healer, however, only one question is truly important. It is what Jesus asked the disciples not long after they had watched him heal a blind man (Mark 8:22–30). "People are all talking about you," the disciples were telling him, "but they can't figure out who you are." Jesus then asked them the question he continues to ask us today: "Who do you say that I am?"

THE KINGDOM IS HERE

Questions to Begin

15 minutes
Use a question or two to get warmed up for the reading.

1 How do you feel when you go back to the town you grew up in?

2 Do your parents really think you are an adult? If you have children eighteen or older, do you see them as adults? Why or why not?

3 What surprised you most at your last high-school reunion?

Opening the Bible

5 minutes
Read the passage aloud. Let individuals take turns reading sections.

The Reading: Isaiah 61:1–3; Luke 4:14–30; 7:18–23

Good News

Isaiah 61:1 The spirit of the Lord GOD is upon me,
    because the LORD has anointed me;
  he has sent me to bring good news to the oppressed,
    to bind up the brokenhearted,
  to proclaim liberty to the captives,
    and release to the prisoners;
  2 to proclaim the year of the LORD's favor,
    and the day of vengeance of our God;
    to comfort all who mourn;
  3 to provide for those who mourn in Zion—
    to give them a garland instead of ashes,
  the oil of gladness instead of mourning,
    the mantle of praise instead of a faint spirit.

Jesus Makes an Announcement

Luke 4:14 Then Jesus, filled with the power of the Spirit, returned to Galilee. . . . 16 When he came to Nazareth, where he had been brought up, he went to the synagogue on the sabbath day, as was his custom. He stood up to read, 17 and the scroll of the prophet Isaiah was given to him. He unrolled the scroll and found the place where it was written:
    18 "The Spirit of the Lord is upon me,
      because he has anointed me
        to bring good news to the poor.
    He has sent me to proclaim release to the captives
      and recovery of sight to the blind,
        to let the oppressed go free,
    19 to proclaim the year of the Lord's favor."
  20 And he rolled up the scroll, gave it back to the attendant, and sat down. The eyes of all in the synagogue were fixed on him. 21 Then he began to say to them, "Today this scripture has been fulfilled in your hearing."

The Crowd Changes Its Mind

22 All spoke well of him and were amazed at the gracious words that came from his mouth. They said, "Is not this Joseph's son?" 23 He said to them, "Doubtless you will quote to me this proverb, 'Doctor, cure yourself!' And you will say, 'Do here also in your hometown the things that we have heard you did at Capernaum.'" 24 And he said, "Truly I tell you, no prophet is accepted in the prophet's hometown. 25 But the truth is, there were many widows in Israel in the time of Elijah, when the heaven was shut up three years and six months, and there was a severe famine over all the land; 26 yet Elijah was sent to none of them except to a widow at Zarephath in Sidon. 27 There were also many lepers in Israel in the time of the prophet Elisha, and none of them was cleansed except Naaman the Syrian." 28 When they heard this, all in the synagogue were filled with rage. 29 They got up, drove him out of the town, and led him to the brow of the hill on which their town was built, so that they might hurl him off the cliff. 30 But he passed through the midst of them and went on his way.

Jesus Answers John the Baptist's Question

Luke 7:18 . . . John summoned two of his disciples 19 and sent them to the Lord to ask, "Are you the one who is to come, or are we to wait for another?" . . . 22 And he answered them, "Go and tell John what you have seen and heard: the blind receive their sight, the lame walk, the lepers are cleansed, the deaf hear, the dead are raised, the poor have good news brought to them. 23 And blessed is anyone who takes no offense at me."

Questions for Careful Reading

10 minutes
Choose questions according to your interest and time.

1 Compare the Isaiah reading with the words Jesus read in the synagogue (Luke 4:18–19). What did Jesus emphasize? What did he leave out? Why do you think he left out parts of the text? After discussing possible reasons, check out John 3:16–17.

2 What kinds of people has the anointed one (Isaiah 61:1) come to help? What do these people have in common?

3 Why did Jesus' audience move from admiration to rage?

4 How do you think Jesus escaped the angry mob?

5 How does Jesus' answer (Luke 7:22) relate to John's question (Luke 7:19)? Would John have been satisfied with it? Could it have reminded John of Isaiah 61? If so, what would he have thought of Jesus?

A Guide to the Reading

If participants have not read this section already, read it aloud. Otherwise go on to "Questions for Application."

Each week we will begin our look at Jesus the healer with some of the most beautiful words in Scripture, poems from the Old Testament prophet Isaiah. In these poems the prophet describes the earth as it should be. God's love reigns over the entire world. There is "liberty and justice for all." Everyone is healthy.

The words are familiar. Many of them are in Handel's great oratorio *Messiah.* Some are read at Mass during the Advent and Christmas seasons. Hearing them today, we may not realize Isaiah's incredible hopefulness. These prophecies were written during a time when Israel was besieged by Assyria and then captured by Babylon. The future was bleak. Without the intervention of a mighty deliverer, God's people were doomed.

Centuries after Isaiah was written, the people of God were once again living under foreign rule. Roman emissaries supervised Jewish priests and petty kings, and people in Judea and Galilee again longed for deliverance. They were not prepared, however, for the announcement a young manual laborer from a remote village was about to make.

Isaiah 61:1–3. The "me" in this poem is the anointed one, the Messiah, God's powerful servant who will restore Israel's fortunes. In the Old Testament, the Messiah is never clearly described. He is powerful, so he may be a king, a prophet, or a warrior. Isaiah's Jewish audience expected the anointed one to rescue them from Babylon and return them to Israel. They believed that when he came, injustice, illness, grief, and pain would end. The early Christians applied this poem to Jesus, whom they called the *Christ,* a Greek word meaning "anointed." Our next reading shows why they made this connection.

Luke 4:14–21. When Jesus was baptized, the Holy Spirit "descended upon him in bodily form like a dove" (Luke 3:22). The Spirit then led him into the wilderness, where he was tempted by the devil (4:1–13). Now, still impelled by the Spirit, Jesus returns to his home turf and begins teaching. *Synagogues* are Jewish places of prayer and study. They may have begun in the sixth century BC while the Jews were captive in Babylon, far from their ruined temple, or they may have begun several centuries later to meet the needs of Jews scattered throughout the Hellenistic empire. By the first century AD most Jewish towns had one, and a guest—or a hometown boy back for a visit—would likely be invited to join the other men by commenting on the day's Scripture portion. But suddenly Jesus does something outrageous: he applies the biblical prophecy to himself. In saying "this scripture has been fulfilled in your hearing," he is saying that he himself is the anointed one!

Luke 4:22–30. At first the listeners don't get it. Everyone murmurs approval of Jesus' words. A common laborer's son from our town, and listen to how well he reads! But then Jesus makes his meaning clear. "Of course you won't accept *me* as the anointed one," he says in effect. "All great prophets have to leave home to get recognition." And then he has the gall to say that he won't perform any miracles for them, and to compare himself with the mighty prophet Elijah, who was miraculously sustained by a poor Lebanese widow (see 1 Kings 17) and who even brought her son back to life, and with Elijah's powerful successor, Elisha, who healed a Syrian warrior of leprosy (see 2 Kings 5)! Suddenly, the crowd turns nasty. Their daughters used to babysit this young man. Who does he think he is? And what gives him the right to insult them, their town, their nation? Stick a fork in this one—he's done. Or so they think.

Luke 7:18–23. John the Baptist is looking for change. He knows the prophecy of Malachi 4:5: "Lo, I will send you the prophet Elijah before the great and terrible day of the Lord comes." Unlike the people of Nazareth, John hopes Jesus is "the one who is to come." But Jesus sends John an unexpected answer. By healing the blind, the lame, the deaf, and people with leprosy, by raising the dead and proclaiming good news to the poor, Jesus identifies himself not with Elijah but with the anointed one, the Messiah described by the prophet Isaiah. Jesus' healing miracles show that the kingdom of God is beginning to burst into human history.

17

Questions for Application

40 minutes
Choose questions according to your interest and time.

1   Have you ever felt called by God
to a particular task, career,
relationship, or way of life? Is it
possible that God is calling and
you haven't noticed? How could
you tune in to the call?

2   Who are the oppressed, broken-
hearted, captives, prisoners, and
mourners in your community?
What is God's good news for
them? Do you have a role in
making the good news happen?

3   Could there be unacknowledged
prophets in your parish? Who
might they be? How can you,
as an individual or with your
small group, help them answer
God's call?

4 Why did Jesus go to the synagogue each week? Why do you (or don't you) go to church regularly?

5 John's disciples ask who Jesus *is.* Jesus responds by telling what he *does.* When people look at what you *do,* what can they tell about who you *are*? Could they guess you are a follower of Jesus? How?

6 What would need to change in your home, your workplace, or your parish to make it more nearly resemble the kingdom of God as Jesus described it? Could any of these changes begin this year?

Participants have a right to know how much time they are investing at a group meeting. The meeting must be kept within strict time limits so that all may plan for other commitments.

Jerome Kodell, O.S.B., *The Catholic Bible Study Handbook*

Approach to Prayer

15 minutes
Use this approach—or create your own!

◆ This prayer is attributed to
St. Teresa of Ávila, a sixteenth-
century Carmelite nun known
for her writings, her reforms,
and her deep spirituality. Pray
it together:

Christ has no body now on earth
    but ours,
no hands but ours, no feet but
    ours.
Ours are the eyes to see the needs
    of the world.
Ours are the hands with which to
    bless everyone now.
Ours are the feet with which he
    is to go about doing good.

Spend a few moments silently
reflecting on what this prayer
means for you. Close with an
Our Father.

A Living Tradition

Healing Like Jesus

This section is a supplement for individual reading.

For two millennia the Church has followed Jesus' example by caring for the sick. Though some miraculous cures have occurred, most Christian health care is quite ordinary— individual Christians tend the sick, the wounded, and the dying; religious orders and lay groups operate hospices and hospitals; dioceses administer health-care institutions. Occasionally, the United States Conference of Catholic Bishops issues a statement to guide the thousands of Catholics involved with health care on a daily basis. These selections are from their 2001 statement.

The bishops point out that Jesus healed the whole person:

Jesus' healing mission went further than caring only for physical affliction. He touched people at the deepest level of their existence; he sought their physical, mental, and spiritual healing (John 6:35, 11:25–27). He "came that they might have life, and have it more abundantly" (John 10:10).

Catholics should, like Jesus, serve those in greatest need:

those people whose social condition puts them at the margins of our society and makes them particularly vulnerable to discrimination: the poor; the uninsured and the underinsured; children and the unborn; single parents; the elderly; those with incurable diseases and chemical dependencies; racial minorities; immigrants and refugees. In particular, the person with mental or physical disabilities, regardless of the cause or severity, must be treated as a unique person of incomparable worth, with the same right to life and to adequate health care as all other persons.

Catholic health care, like Jesus' healing work, is a sign of God's coming kingdom:

Catholic health care services rejoice in the challenge to be Christ's healing compassion in the world and see their ministry not only as an effort to restore and preserve health but also as a spiritual service and a sign of that final healing that will one day bring about the new creation that is the ultimate fruit of Jesus' ministry and God's love for us.

The entire statement can be read online at http://www.usccb.org/bishops/directives.htm.

Signs of the Kingdom

Questions to Begin

15 minutes
Use a question or two to get warmed up for the reading.

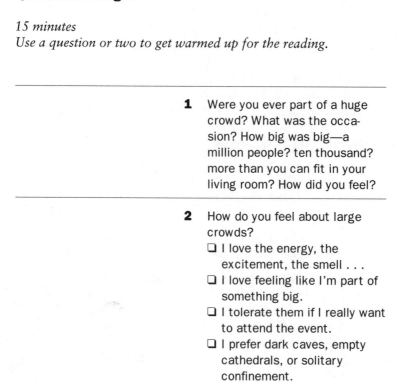

1   Were you ever part of a huge crowd? What was the occasion? How big was big—a million people? ten thousand? more than you can fit in your living room? How did you feel?

2   How do you feel about large crowds?
❑ I love the energy, the excitement, the smell . . .
❑ I love feeling like I'm part of something big.
❑ I tolerate them if I really want to attend the event.
❑ I prefer dark caves, empty cathedrals, or solitary confinement.

Opening the Bible

5 minutes
Read the passage aloud. Let individuals take turns reading sections.

The Reading: Isaiah 35:5–6; Mark 1:40–45; 7:32–37; 8:22–30

Joy in the Kingdom

Isaiah 35:5 Then the eyes of the blind shall be opened,
     and the ears of the deaf unstopped;
6 then the lame shall leap like a deer,
     and the tongue of the speechless sing for joy.

A Victim of Leprosy

Mark 1:40 A leper came to him begging him, and kneeling he said to him, "If you choose, you can make me clean." 41 Moved with pity, Jesus stretched out his hand and touched him, and said to him, "I do choose. Be made clean!" 42 Immediately the leprosy left him, and he was made clean. 43 After sternly warning him he sent him away at once, 44 saying to him, "See that you say nothing to anyone; but go, show yourself to the priest, and offer for your cleansing what Moses commanded, as a testimony to them." 45 But he went out and began to proclaim it freely, and to spread the word, so that Jesus could no longer go into a town openly, but stayed out in the country; and people came to him from every quarter.

A Deaf Man and a Blind Man

Mark 7:32 They brought to him a deaf man who had an impediment in his speech; and they begged him to lay his hand on him. 33 He took him aside in private, away from the crowd, and put his fingers into his ears, and he spat and touched his tongue. 34 Then looking up to heaven, he sighed and said to him, "Ephphatha," that is, "Be opened." 35 And immediately his ears were opened, his tongue was released, and he spoke plainly. 36 Then Jesus ordered them to tell no one; but the more he ordered them, the more zealously they proclaimed it. 37 They were astounded beyond measure, saying, "He has done everything well; he even makes the deaf to hear and the mute to speak."

Mark 8:22 They came to Bethsaida. Some people brought a blind man to him and begged him to touch him. 23 He took the blind man by the hand and led him out of the village; and when he had put saliva on his eyes and laid his hands on him, he asked him, "Can you see anything?" 24 And the man looked up and said, "I can see people, but they look like trees, walking." 25 Then Jesus laid his hands on his eyes again; and he looked intently and his sight was restored, and he saw everything clearly. 26 Then he sent him away to his home, saying, "Do not even go into the village."

"Who Am I?"

27 Jesus went on with his disciples to the villages of Caesarea Philippi; and on the way he asked his disciples, "Who do people say that I am?" 28 And they answered him, "John the Baptist; and others, Elijah; and still others, one of the prophets." 29 He asked them, "But who do you say that I am?" Peter answered him, "You are the Messiah." 30 And he sternly ordered them not to tell anyone about him.

10 minutes
Choose questions according to your interest and time.

1 How do the leper, the blind man, and the deaf man (or their friends) approach Jesus? What does this say about their attitude toward Jesus?

begging

2 What does the leper know Jesus can do? What is he less sure about?

make him clean

if he wants to

3 Why does Jesus touch people as part of the healing process? (Brainstorm this one: there may be quite a few reasons.)

There needs to be contact

4 In these readings we see Jesus' power over illness—at his command, the illness leaves. What command of his is consistently disobeyed? What is the result?

be quiet
Tell no one

5 How do you think Peter knows Jesus' true identity? Refer to Week 1 for some ideas.

A Guide to the Reading

*If participants have not read this section already, read it aloud.
Otherwise go on to "Questions for Application."*

L ast week we heard Jesus announce God's kingdom, first in
his hometown and then to John the Baptist. Now we are
seeing Jesus in action. What happens when God's kingdom
breaks into this world?

Isaiah 35:5–6. Isaiah 35 shows nature rejoicing as
God's people return from captivity. When God restores his people,
he restores everything—earth along with heaven, body along with
soul. Why does Jesus open the eyes of the blind and the ears of the
deaf? Why does he raise the dead, restore speech to the speech-
less, and send the lame dancing on their way? These healings are
not magical tricks meant to show off his great power. Jesus does
not do magic: not for the devil (see Luke 4:1–13), not for religious
leaders (Matthew 12:38–39), not for King Herod (Luke 23:6–9).
Jesus heals because the kingdom of God is present.

Mark 1:40–45. In the ancient world, leprosy—a term
that covered a variety of skin diseases—was greatly feared. The
law of Moses required lepers to wear torn clothes, live apart from
others, and cry "Unclean!" when passing through town (Leviticus
13:45–46). Anyone who touched a leper risked not only contagion
but also temporary isolation from the community. Occasionally,
leprosy went into remission. When that happened, a priest could
certify that the leper, now clean, could safely return to normal life.

Jesus must have shocked the onlookers. First, he volun-
tarily touches the leper. Then the leprosy disappears. In the words
of the fourth-century preacher St. John Chrysostom, "He touched
the leper to signify that he heals not as servant but as Lord. For
the leprosy did not defile his hand, but his holy hand cleansed the
leprous body." Something unheard-of has just taken place, but
Jesus does not want publicity. Of course, once the leper is certified
clean and back in the community, publicity is inevitable.

Mark 7:32–37; 8:22–26. Jesus says "Be opened" to
the man, not just to his ears or mouth. In God's kingdom, healing
is for the whole person, not just the malfunctioning parts. When
the people say Jesus has "done everything well," they are echoing
the refrain in the creation story: "God saw everything that he had

made, and indeed, it was very good" (Genesis 1:31). We enter into God's new creation through baptism, and part of the baptismal liturgy comes from this story. In a rite called the ephphatha, the priest blesses the catechumen's or the child's ears and mouth so that they may be open to hearing and proclaiming God's word.

In the Church's sacrament of prayer for the sick, the priest imitates Jesus by laying hands on the sick person, though he anoints with oil rather than saliva. (Greek and Jewish healers in the ancient world often used saliva; at least it was always available.) We can take courage from the fact that it takes two tries before the blind man sees clearly. It takes many more than two lessons for Jesus' followers to see and understand the nature of God's kingdom. Fortunately, Jesus keeps trying!

Mark 8:27–30. By healing the leper, the blind man, and the deaf man, Jesus fulfills three of the signs he has given John the Baptist as evidence of God's kingdom (Luke 7:18–23). Next week we'll look at another sign: raising a dead girl to life. Each time, Jesus asks the onlookers for silence. Does he not want people to know the kingdom is coming and he is the Messiah?

Most likely he does not want the miracles misunderstood. Plenty of people are eager to follow a wonder-worker who will entertain them and make them feel better at the same time. Few want to follow a Messiah who will willingly suffer and die. Even the disciples don't catch on. Though Peter affirms that Jesus is the Messiah, he does not want to hear Jesus talk about death (see 8:31–33). Jesus may be hoping to downplay the miracles until after his death and resurrection, when people can better understand what kind of kingdom he is establishing.

Questions for Application

40 minutes
Choose questions according to your interest and time.

1 Imagine you are living in Galilee two thousand years ago. You have heard stories about a young tradesman who can heal people. You know he isn't a doctor or a priest. What do you think? What will you do? What would make you believe he is from God?

2 Have you ever begged Jesus for anything? What happened?

3 The leper says to Jesus, "If you choose, you can make me clean" (Mark 1:40). Do you believe Jesus can heal the sick today? Do you believe he chooses to? How do your beliefs affect your prayers?

4 People bring the deaf man and the blind man to Jesus; the leper comes on his own. Are you comfortable going to Jesus on your own? If not, who can bring you? Is there someone you should bring? How is this done today?

5 Not all healing is instantaneous. The blind man is healed in stages. Is God in the process of healing something in your life? When did the process begin? Where is it now?

6 There are lots of books and movies about Jesus nowadays, each with a different idea of who he is. Who do you say he is? Why?

Effective small groups focus not only upon ideas but on how people feel about those ideas.

Richard Price, Pat Springle, and Joe Kloba, *Rapha's Handbook for Group Leaders*

Approach to Prayer

15 minutes
Use one of these approaches—or create your own!

♦ Spend a few moments silently thinking of loved ones who are in need of healing.

Leader: *Lord, if you choose, you can make us whole. We bring you these people we love, knowing that you love them even more than we do:*

Individuals may name loved ones or may simply say "a friend," "a relative," "the woman in the next cubicle," or whatever feels comfortable and will not betray any confidences. After each name, the group responds:

Lord, have mercy.

Conclude with a Glory to the Father.

♦ Ask someone to read Psalm 145, a praise poem about God's wonderful kingdom.

Saints in the Making

Unclean!

This section is a supplement for individual reading.

Nowadays, leprosy (Hansen's disease) can be halted with antibiotics, and it is virtually unknown in North America and Europe. Once, however, it was considered a fate worse than death. Not only did lepers suffer from a then-incurable wasting disease; they also had to deal with the community's fear of infection. A diagnosis of leprosy turned a person into a pariah. Lepers could never again sit down with their families for dinner or walk through town without calling out a warning. Some medieval churches installed low windows so lepers could watch the Mass without contacting other parishioners.

No wonder saints were often identified by their kindness to lepers. In the fifth century St. Brigid of Ireland incurred her father's wrath by giving his sword to a leper. In the thirteenth century the young St. Francis of Assisi, overcoming his own revulsion, leaped off his horse and kissed a leper. Perhaps more important, the Church established hundreds of leprosariums around the world, and countless religious and laypeople devoted their lives to serving these feared and abandoned sufferers.

One of these dedicated Christians was a young Belgian priest, Father Damien de Veuster, who in 1873 volunteered to work in a leper colony on the Hawaiian island of Molokai. Nine years later he was diagnosed with the disease, dying in 1889 at age forty-nine. At his request a group of Franciscan sisters from New York led by Mother Marianne Cope took over the work among the island's one thousand lepers. They could not heal the lepers, but they could wash their wounds, grow fresh fruits and vegetables, care for their children, and make their lives more pleasant with games and music.

Hansen's disease today occurs in only a few countries, mostly among the poorest of the poor. Over half the world's sufferers are in India, where the late Mother Teresa and her Missionaries of Charity founded Shanti Nagar ("Town of Peace"), a leper colony. She reportedly urged Pope John Paul II to canonize Father Damien. The necessary miracle for authenticating his sainthood, she said, could be found in Father Damien's influence, which has contributed toward today's humane treatment of people with leprosy. The pope declared Father Damien "blessed"—a stage toward canonization—in 1995.

No More Weeping

Questions to Begin

15 minutes
Use a question or two to get warmed up for the reading.

1 How old do you think you'll live to be? Why?

2 Who handles pain better—men or women?

3 When you are ill (not with the stomach flu!), what do you want to eat?

5 minutes
Read the passage aloud. Let individuals take turns reading
sections.

The Reading: Isaiah 65:17–20; Mark 5:21–43

New Heavens, New Earth

Isaiah 65:17 For I am about to create new heavens
    and a new earth;
  the former things shall not be remembered
    or come to mind.
18 But be glad and rejoice forever
    in what I am creating;
  for I am about to create Jerusalem as a joy,
    and its people as a delight.
19 I will rejoice in Jerusalem,
    and delight in my people;
  no more shall the sound of weeping be heard in it,
    or the cry of distress.
20 No more shall there be in it
    an infant that lives but a few days,
    or an old person who does not live out a lifetime;
  for one who dies at a hundred years will be considered
    a youth,
  and one who falls short of a hundred will be
    considered accursed.

A Frantic Father

Mark 5:21 When Jesus had crossed again in the boat to the other side, a great crowd gathered around him; and he was by the sea. 22 Then one of the leaders of the synagogue named Jairus came and, when he saw him, fell at his feet 23 and begged him repeatedly, "My little daughter is at the point of death. Come and lay your hands on her, so that she may be made well, and live." 24 So he went with him.

And a large crowd followed him and pressed in on him.

A Desperate Woman

25 Now there was a woman who had been suffering from hemorrhages for twelve years. 26 She had endured much under many physicians, and had spent all that she had; and she was no better, but rather grew worse. 27 She had heard about Jesus, and came up behind him in the

crowd and touched his cloak, 28 for she said, "If I but touch his clothes, I will be made well." 29 Immediately her hemorrhage stopped; and she felt in her body that she was healed of her disease. 30 Immediately aware that power had gone forth from him, Jesus turned about in the crowd and said, "Who touched my clothes?" 31 And his disciples said to him, "You see the crowd pressing in on you; how can you say, 'Who touched me?'" 32 He looked all around to see who had done it. 33 But the woman, knowing what had happened to her, came in fear and trembling, fell down before him, and told him the whole truth. 34 He said to her, "Daughter, your faith has made you well; go in peace, and be healed of your disease."

An Amazing Wake

35 While he was still speaking, some people came from the leader's house to say, "Your daughter is dead. Why trouble the teacher any further?" 36 But overhearing what they said, Jesus said to the leader of the synagogue, "Do not fear, only believe." 37 He allowed no one to follow him except Peter, James, and John, the brother of James. 38 When they came to the house of the leader of the synagogue, he saw a commotion, people weeping and wailing loudly. 39 When he had entered, he said to them, "Why do you make a commotion and weep? The child is not dead but sleeping." 40 And they laughed at him. Then he put them all outside, and took the child's father and mother and those who were with him, and went in where the child was. 41 He took her by the hand and said to her, "Talitha cum," which means, "Little girl, get up!" 42 And immediately the girl got up and began to walk about (she was twelve years of age). At this they were overcome with amazement. 43 He strictly ordered them that no one should know this, and told them to give her something to eat.

10 minutes
Choose questions according to your interest and time.

1 What makes the "new heavens and a new earth" (Isaiah 65:17) different from the earth as we know it?

2 Which details of the story show that Jairus is desperate? What do you think is going through his mind when the woman slows down the procession?

3 Why does Jesus ask who touched his clothes? Does he want information, or something else?

4 Does touching Jesus' clothes heal the woman? If so, how? If not, what does?

5 Do you think Jairus's daughter was really dead? Why or why not?

A Guide to the Reading

If participants have not read this section already, read it aloud. Otherwise go on to "Questions for Application."

Isaiah 65:17–20. If you have time, read the rest of this chapter (verses 21–25) aloud. What a beautiful picture Isaiah paints of the world as it was created to be, and as it will be one day when "the kingdom of the world has become the kingdom of our Lord and of his Messiah" (Revelation 11:15)! The author of the New Testament book of Revelation alludes to Isaiah's poem in his description of "a new heaven and a new earth." "God himself will be with them," he writes. "He will wipe every tear from their eyes. Death will be no more; mourning and crying and pain will be no more, for the first things have passed away" (Revelation 21:1–4).

Mark 5:21–24. Back in Galilee, an influential religious leader is in anguish—his little girl is dying. Most accounts of Jesus' healing miracles provide no names. A leper, a blind man, a deaf man, a Canaanite woman . . . these people emerge briefly from the ever-present crowd, receive their healing, and recede into anonymity. Not so Jairus. He is well known in his community, and for him, coming to Jesus could mean public humiliation. What if Jesus says no? What if the stories about Jesus' healing power are exaggerated, and Jesus is unable to help the child? Jairus does not stop to doubt. He not only begs Jesus to come, he does so repeatedly.

Mark 5:25–34. But just as Jairus is beginning to hope, the procession stops. "Who touched my clothes?" Jesus asks, and a cowering woman comes forward to identify herself. For twelve years she has looked for a cure, to no avail. Now, broke and desperate, she turns to Jesus. It isn't just that she is in pain, though a twelve-year hemorrhage can't be pleasant. According to the law of Leviticus, she is ritually unclean. Anyone who touches her—even accidentally—must bathe, wash his clothes, and keep away from people until evening (see Leviticus 15:25–27).

Convinced she can be healed if she touches Jesus' garment, she hopes to pass unnoticed in the crowd. But Jesus is not a magician. His clothes do not heal people; his love does. Rather than scold her or jump back in horror when he realizes an "unclean" woman has touched him, he commends her for her faith and assures her that she is healed.

Mark 5:35–43. Meanwhile, precious time is passing. Suddenly, messengers arrive with the news Jairus dreads: his daughter has died. All hope drains away. Jarius knows Jesus can heal, but does he dare ask him to raise a dead girl? His messengers want him to give up; they think it's too late for Jesus to make a difference. But Jesus insists on continuing down the road. Similarly, many scholars accept that Jesus healed the sick, but some have trouble believing he could bring dead people back to life.

In this case, Jesus offers an apparent out: he says that the child is sleeping. Was she not dead but in a deep coma? It can't be proved one way or the other, of course. For a time, however, everyone was sure she was dead—the messengers, her father and mother, the people already assembled to mourn for her. They were so sure, in fact, that they ridicule Jesus for suggesting anything else.

The Gospels tell of one other occasion when Jesus says a dead person is sleeping: when he raises Lazarus, who has been dead for four days and has already started to decompose (John 11). Death, for Jesus, is a sleep, not a permanent state. It does not mean the end of all hope. It does not limit the kingdom of God. Just as Jesus restores sight to the blind, makes the lame walk, cleanses lepers, makes the deaf hear, and brings good news to the poor, he also raises the dead (Luke 7:22). And then he orders the crowd to be quiet, because it is not yet time for him to reveal the nature of the kingdom. As if anyone who saw a dead girl get out of bed, walk, and eat lunch could keep quiet about it!

Questions for Application

40 minutes
Choose questions according to your interest and time.

1 According to the books of Isaiah and Revelation, there will be no weeping in the new earth. Why do we weep now? What will be different then?

2 A synagogue leader kneels before a manual laborer . . . An "unclean" woman sneaks up and touches a well-known wonder-worker . . . How does your self-image affect how you come to Jesus, or whether you come at all?

3 After twelve years of suffering, the woman has nearly given up hope. Do you have any long-term problems that still need healing? Is it too late to ask for help? If the woman had decided just to live with her problem, would she have been healed?

4 Mark 5:30 says that "power had gone forth from him." How do you define power? In this case, what does Jesus' power do? When is power bad? When is it good?

5 Jairus must have panicked when Jesus stopped to heal the woman. Is some aspect of your life moving too slowly? How might this story help you trust in God's timing?

6 The last detail of the story— "and told them to give her something to eat"—shows Jesus' personal care for the little girl. Do we, in our hurry, neglect the little details that make people feel loved? What could you do tomorrow to show one person that you care?

Out of our experience of the word, enlightened by the Holy Spirit, we speak the word to one another.

M. Basil Pennington, O.C.S.O., *Seeking His Mind*

Approach to Prayer

15 minutes
Use one or both of these approaches—or create your own!

◆ Ask someone to read these words from Thomas Merton:

Perfect hope is achieved on the brink of despair when, instead of falling over the edge, we find ourselves walking on the air. Hope is always just about to turn into despair, but never does so, for at the moment of supreme crisis God's power is suddenly made perfect in our infirmity. So we learn to expect His mercy most calmly when all is most dangerous, to seek Him quietly in the face of peril, certain that He cannot fail us though we may be upbraided by the just and rejected by those who claim to hold the evidence of His love.

Pause for a few moments of silent reflection. If you sense danger in your life right now, picture yourself going through it with Jesus at your side. If things are going well for you, give thanks for the blessings you enjoy. Close with a Hail Mary.

◆ As you may have done last week, remember loved ones in need of healing. The group may respond with "Lord, have mercy" after each intention is spoken.

Saints in the Making

Women and Girls at Lourdes

This section is a supplement for individual reading.

L ourdes, a village in southwestern France, was turned upside down in 1858 when a fourteen-year-old resident, Bernadette Soubirous, saw the Blessed Virgin. Immediately, people began flocking to the spring where the apparitions were occurring. Several reported miraculous healings. A century and a half later, an estimated six million people come to Lourdes every year. Some believe they are healed through the Virgin's intercession. The Church has carefully examined thousands of healings and, as of 1999, has recognized sixty-six as definitely miraculous. Fifty-three of those sixty-six have been women or girls.

At age sixty-four, Sister Marie-Marguerite had endured deteriorating health for thirteen years—chronic kidney disease, frequent angina attacks, severe edema in her legs. By 1937 her community believed she was dying, and the sisters prayed a novena—a prayer repeated for nine days—to Our Lady of Lourdes. On the last day of the novena during Mass, just as the Host was elevated, her pain suddenly disappeared. Her swollen legs returned to normal size so quickly that the bandages fell off. The next day she resumed her normal work at the convent, which she kept doing for the next eight years.

Delizia Cirolli was only eleven when her right knee began hurting. Exploratory surgery revealed a malignant tumor. Her doctor advised amputation and radiation therapy, but her parents feared she could not tolerate hospitalization. Delizia's teacher persuaded her mother to take her to Lourdes—a journey of more than fifteen hundred miles from their Sicilian home. In August 1976 the two of them made the trip, but when they returned home, Delizia's condition deteriorated. Now bedridden, she feared she would soon be completely paralyzed. However, she and her mother continued to pray. Several months passed; Delizia turned twelve. In December she nearly stopped eating, and her mother began to make her burial dress. Then, just before Christmas, Delizia suddenly felt better. She got out of bed and went outside for a walk. The pain totally disappeared, and in January she returned to school. Today, Delizia's faith is strong. She works as an obstetrical nurse and makes a yearly pilgrimage to Lourdes.

FAITH AMONG THE PAGANS

Questions to Begin

15 minutes
Use a question or two to get warmed up for the reading.

---

1 Are you good at delegating? What task is hard for you to let go of?

---

2 If the boss says no to something you really need, how do you change his or her mind?

---

3 What is your pet's favorite kind of people food?

Opening the Bible

5 minutes
Read the passage aloud. Let individuals take turns reading sections.

The Reading: Isaiah 49:5–6; Matthew 8:5–13; 15:21–31

A Light to the Nations

Isaiah 49:5 And now the LORD says,
>who formed me in the womb to be his servant,
to bring Jacob back to him,
>and that Israel might be gathered to him, . . .

6 "It is too light a thing that you should be my servant
>to raise up the tribes of Jacob
and to restore the survivors of Israel;
I will give you as a light to the nations,
>that my salvation may reach to the end of the earth."

A Faithful Military Officer

Matthew 8:5 When he entered Capernaum, a centurion came to him, appealing to him 6 and saying, "Lord, my servant is lying at home paralyzed, in terrible distress." 7 And he said to him, "I will come and cure him." 8 The centurion answered, "Lord, I am not worthy to have you come under my roof; but only speak the word, and my servant will be healed. 9 For I also am a man under authority, with soldiers under me; and I say to one, 'Go,' and he goes, and to another, 'Come,' and he comes, and to my slave, 'Do this,' and the slave does it." 10 When Jesus heard him, he was amazed and said to those who followed him, "Truly I tell you, in no one in Israel have I found such faith. 11 I tell you, many will come from east and west and will eat with Abraham and Isaac and Jacob in the kingdom of heaven, 12 while the heirs of the kingdom will be thrown into the outer darkness, where there will be weeping and gnashing of teeth." 13 And to the centurion Jesus said, "Go; let it be done for you according to your faith." And the servant was healed in that hour.

A Persistent Canaanite Mother

Matthew 15:21 Jesus left that place and went away to the district of Tyre and Sidon. 22 Just then a Canaanite woman from that region came out and started shouting, "Have mercy on me, Lord, Son of David; my daughter is tormented by a demon." 23 But he did not

43

answer her at all. And his disciples came and urged him, saying, "Send her away, for she keeps shouting after us." 24 He answered, "I was sent only to the lost sheep of the house of Israel." 25 But she came and knelt before him, saying, "Lord, help me." 26 He answered, "It is not fair to take the children's food and throw it to the dogs." 27 She said, "Yes, Lord, yet even the dogs eat the crumbs that fall from their masters' table." 28 Then Jesus answered her, "Woman, great is your faith! Let it be done for you as you wish." And her daughter was healed instantly.

Praise to the God of Israel

29 After Jesus had left that place, he passed along the Sea of Galilee, and he went up the mountain, where he sat down. 30 Great crowds came to him, bringing with them the lame, the maimed, the blind, the mute, and many others. They put them at his feet, and he cured them, 31 so that the crowd was amazed when they saw the mute speaking, the maimed whole, the lame walking, and the blind seeing. And they praised the God of Israel.

Questions for Careful Reading

10 minutes
Choose questions according to your interest and time.

1 In the Isaiah reading, what was the prophet born to do? How does his job description expand?

2 What do the centurion and the Canaanite woman have in common?   *Faith*

3 How does the centurion's speech about delegation show his faith? What does he expect Jesus to have authority over?

4 What do Jesus and the Canaanite woman mean by their talk about animals—lost sheep (Matthew 15:24) and begging dogs (Matthew 15:26–27)?

5 The crowd described in Matthew 15:31 responds differently from the people in Nazareth (Week 1, Luke 4:22–30). What's the difference between the two groups?

A Guide to the Reading

If participants have not read this section already, read it aloud. Otherwise go on to "Questions for Application."

Isaiah 49:5–6. God's servant is on a mission, not only to restore God's people but also to offer salvation to the entire world. We tend to think of *salvation* as a purely religious word, one that has to do with life after death. That's only part of the story. The Hebrew word for salvation used here also means deliverance, safety, well-being, and health. God's servant will bring wholeness to everyone, gentiles as well as Jews.

Matthew 8:5–13. Soldiers are a familiar sight in Capernaum, a Galilean town bordering the territories of two petty kings. The centurion, a military commander, has lived among Jews long enough to understand their taboos. He knows a Jew will not want to go home with him. If he invites Jesus into his living room, he will be polite and offer him food and drink. But if Jesus accepts refreshments—and it would be rude not to—he will be in danger of breaking ritual purity laws.

The centurion does not let the roadblocks stop him. His servant needs help. He will ask for a remote miracle. But before he can finish his carefully crafted appeal, Jesus interrupts and offers to go to his house. Surprised, the centurion continues with his original speech: "You don't need to come with me. You have as much authority over illness as I have over the soldiers in my command. When you speak, illness obeys." Now it is Jesus' turn to be surprised. This man is showing what faith means—conviction that Jesus has the power and the desire to make people whole. Next time you receive communion, remember the centurion as you repeat the words of faith based on his appeal: "Lord, I am not worthy to receive you, but only say the word and I shall be healed."

Matthew 15:21–28. Jesus is on the road to Lebanon when a pagan woman accosts him. She clearly knows something about Jewish tradition: she calls him "Son of David," a Jewish term for the expected messiah. She no doubt expects that, as a Jewish man, he will not wish to speak to a woman or a gentile. And indeed he ignores her—so she keeps shouting. Eventually he speaks, and if what he says offends our supposedly tolerant, inclusive ears, imagine how it sounds to a woman pleading for her child's life. Sent only to Israel, he says? And just who are you calling a dog?

The disciples are relieved. They know Jesus' mission is to Israel—that's what he told them not so long ago when he sent them out to heal (Matthew 10:1–6). They don't waste any love on gentiles, especially female ones. Now maybe this noisy woman will go away. But wait . . . what's going on? The woman is kneeling, pleading, saying she's willing to eat crumbs. And Jesus is agreeing to heal her daughter, a mere gentile girl! After what he's said, how can he do this?

As Isaiah had foretold, the Lord's servant will restore the whole world, from Israel to the ends of the earth. The disciples do not understand this until some time after Jesus' resurrection. Yet this gentile woman understands: when the children are well fed, the entire household—right down to the puppies under the table—feast with them.

Matthew 15:29–31. The Gospels are not anti-Semitic. Jesus is a Jew. His disciples are Jews. Most of the people he heals are Jews. And when he heals gentiles, the onlookers—Jews and gentiles alike—"praised the God of Israel." When Jesus talks about gentiles "in the kingdom of heaven" and Jews in "outer darkness" (Matthew 8:11–12), he is expressing frustration. His ultimate mission is to gather Jews and gentiles together in God's kingdom. As a Jew, he feels especially hurt when any of his own people reject him, and he is delighted and maybe even surprised whenever a gentile shows faith. Don't get the impression from this week's reading that most of Jesus' adherents are gentiles. Though gentile Christians will eventually outnumber Jewish Christians, the great majority of Jesus' early followers are Jews. God has chosen Israel, and through Israel God's kingdom will come.

Questions for Application

40 minutes
Choose questions according to your interest and time.

---

1   Jesus commends the centurion and the Canaanite woman for their faith. If you had to define faith based only on these two stories, what would you say it is? Do you have this kind of faith?

---

2   The centurion and the Canaanite woman are gentiles, and yet Jesus says their faith is greater than that of many of the people of God. Is there a connection between your religious affiliation and your faith in God? What's positive about it? What's negative?

---

3   The centurion says he is not worthy of having Jesus enter his house. Do you ever feel unworthy? Should unworthiness stop you from approaching Jesus?

4   What is the connection between faith and healing? Does the servant or the Canaanite child have faith? Does the centurion's or the mother's faith heal the sick people? If not, what does?

5   Is it possible for our prayers to be too polite? What would have happened if the Canaanite woman had accepted Jesus' first statement at face value? How does Jesus respond to her spunk? Will this story make a difference in the way you pray?

6   In the Sermon on the Mount, Jesus says, "Let your light shine before others, so that they may see your good works and give glory to your Father in heaven" (Matthew 5:16). What kinds of "good works" attract attention to God?

Small groups provide a way of transcending our most self-centered interests; they temper our individualism and our culturally induced desire to be totally independent of one another.

Robert Wuthnow, *Sharing the Journey*

Approach to Prayer

15 minutes
Use one or both of these approaches—or create your own!

◆ Ask someone to read these words from Mother Teresa of Calcutta:

There is no great difference in reality between one country and another, because it is always people you meet everywhere. They may look different or be dressed differently, or may have a different education or position; but they are all the same. They are all people to be loved; they are all hungry for love.

Sit quietly for a few minutes, keeping your eyes closed. Visualize someone you have encountered today who seems quite different from you. Picture Jesus talking with him or her. What does the person ask of Jesus? How does he respond? Now picture Jesus turning to you. What does he say? Close with an Our Father.

◆ Continue remembering loved ones in need of healing. The group may respond with "Lord, have mercy" after each intention. Have prayers been answered? Consider sharing this with the group.

Saints in the Making

When Christ Is Present

This section is a supplement for individual reading.

Father Richard Bain, now a hospital chaplain, was for many years director of the healing ministry of the Roman Catholic Archdiocese of San Francisco. While a seminary student in the seventies, he attended a healing service led by Francis MacNutt, who told would-be healers to pray that their hands would become the hands of Jesus. Bain tried praying this way as he laid hands on some shut-ins he was visiting—and was surprised a few days later when several of them told him their arthritis had significantly improved.

Since that time, Father Bain has prayed for hundreds of thousands of people throughout the United States. Many claim to have been healed of serious diseases including Alzheimer's, cancer, diabetes, and epilepsy. Though some of these healings are no doubt due to the placebo effect, Father Bain estimates that a fourth to a third result from God's direct intervention. Nevertheless, he does not consider himself a miracle worker. In a Web site article on healing Masses he writes:

At the beginning of the Mass, I explain that if we have come to receive a healing, then nothing will happen, because there is no one present with an extraordinary gift of healing; but if we have come to pray, then great things will happen, because when we pray the prayer of the Church, the Holy Sacrifice of the Mass, Christ is always present, and when Christ is present, his love is present, and when his love is present, healings take place. It is Our Lord's deep compassionate and unconditional love that heals us.

Not everyone who comes to Father Bain is healed. He has had to cut back his own schedule for health reasons. But whether or not physical healing occurs, he says, "everyone is changed by the experience of a healing Mass." People leave with renewed faith, with the assurance that they are in God's loving hands whatever the future holds.

Reporters describe Father Bain as "humble" and "self-effacing." Far from calling attention to himself, he continually points people to prayer, to the Eucharist, and to Jesus Christ. As a healer in Jesus' name, he is confident that Jesus will give each praying person the gift that he or she most needs.

BEYOND FAITH AND HOPE

Questions to Begin

15 minutes
Use a question or two to get warmed up for the reading.

1 What's the scariest movie you've ever seen?

2 What did you do for Halloween when you were a teenager?

3 How do you respond when street people ask you for money?

Opening the Bible

5 minutes
Read the passage aloud. Let individuals take turns reading sections.

The Reading: Isaiah 58:6–9; Mark 5:1–20

Loosing the Bonds, Freeing the Oppressed

Isaiah 58:6 Is not this the fast that I choose:
     to loose the bonds of injustice,
     to undo the thongs of the yoke,
   to let the oppressed go free,
     and to break every yoke?
7 Is it not to share your bread with the hungry,
     and bring the homeless poor into your house;
  when you see the naked, to cover them,
     and not to hide yourself from your own kin?
8 Then your light shall break forth like the dawn,
     and your healing shall spring up quickly . . .
9 Then you shall call, and the LORD will answer;
     you shall cry for help, and he will say, Here I am.

A Wild Man in the Graveyard

Mark 5:1 They came to the other side of the sea, to the country of the Gerasenes. 2 And when he had stepped out of the boat, immediately a man out of the tombs with an unclean spirit met him. 3 He lived among the tombs; and no one could restrain him any more, even with a chain; 4 for he had often been restrained with shackles and chains, but the chains he wrenched apart, and the shackles he broke in pieces; and no one had the strength to subdue him. 5 Night and day among the tombs and on the mountains he was always howling and bruising himself with stones.

Jesus Banishes the Demons

6 When he saw Jesus from a distance, he ran and bowed down before him; 7 and he shouted at the top of his voice, "What have you to do with me, Jesus, Son of the Most High God? I adjure you by God, do not torment me." 8 For he had said to him, "Come out of the man, you unclean spirit!" 9 Then Jesus asked him, "What is your name?" He replied, "My name is Legion; for we are many." 10 He begged him earnestly not to send them out of the country. 11 Now there on the hillside a great herd of swine was feeding; 12 and the unclean spirits

begged him, "Send us into the swine; let us enter them." 13 So he gave them permission. And the unclean spirits came out and entered the swine; and the herd, numbering about two thousand, rushed down the steep bank into the sea, and were drowned in the sea.

Tell Everyone What the Lord Has Done

14 The swineherds ran off and told it in the city and in the country. Then people came to see what it was that had happened. 15 They came to Jesus and saw the demoniac sitting there, clothed and in his right mind, the very man who had had the legion; and they were afraid. 16 Those who had seen what had happened to the demoniac and to the swine reported it. 17 Then they began to beg Jesus to leave their neighborhood. 18 As he was getting into the boat, the man who had been possessed by demons begged him that he might be with him. 19 But Jesus refused, and said to him, "Go home to your friends, and tell them how much the Lord has done for you, and what mercy he has shown you." 20 And he went away and began to proclaim in the Decapolis how much Jesus had done for him; and everyone was amazed.

Questions for Careful Reading

10 minutes
Choose questions according to your interest and time.

1 What groups of people does Isaiah tell God's people to serve? What will be the result?

2 Which of the groups described by Isaiah might include the man in the graveyard? Has anybody tried to help him? How?

3 Who speaks to Jesus? What is the speaker's attitude?

4 What effect would the stampede (Mark 5:13) have had on the people in the surrounding towns?

5 Contrast the demon-possessed man's life before and after he meets Jesus.

A Guide to the Reading

If participants have not read this section already, read it aloud. Otherwise go on to "Questions for Application."

Isaiah 58:6–9. Do you want healing? help? answered prayers? Don't give up food, says the prophet. Give up selfishness. Imagine a world with no corrupt judges or unfair laws, no oppressed minorities, no slavery or inadequate wages, no hunger, no homelessness; a world where people see other people's needs and do what they can to meet them, where families are havens for the helpless and nobody is ever turned away. That is what the kingdom of God looks like.

Mark 5:1–5. The man in this story is far from God's kingdom. The Talmud, a collection of Jewish traditions, lists four signs of insanity: "spending the night in a grave, tearing one's clothes, walking around at night, and destroying anything given." That's our man. In addition to being insane, he lives in a graveyard, next door to a—shudder—pig farm. And, of course, he has an unclean spirit. In other words, he is demon possessed.

Until recently, people didn't know much about epilepsy, Tourette's syndrome, multiple personality disorder, schizophrenia, or any of the hundreds of illnesses that can make people behave in unusual ways. A lot of people have been said to be demon possessed when actually they were victims of disease. Jesus healed many of these people along with the deaf, the lame, and the blind. But the man in this story goes way beyond illness.

In his 1983 book *People of the Lie,* psychiatrist M. Scott Peck looks at the connection between demon possession and mental illness. Most mentally ill people are not demon possessed, according to Peck, but all demon-possessed people are also mentally ill. "There has to be a significant emotional problem for the possession to occur in the first place," he writes. "Then the possession itself will both enhance that problem and create new ones." The man in the tombs has more than his share of emotional problems.

Mark 5:6–13. Jesus does not treat this situation like one that demands ordinary healing. When Jesus heals sick people, even many of the ones said to be demon possessed, he usually speaks either to the suffering person or to the person's caregiver. By contrast, when Jesus sees this man running toward him, he speaks directly to the demons. The demons are clearly frightened of Jesus. They try to get power over him by shouting his name. They show they have supernatural knowledge by calling him "Son of the Most High God," something his own disciples haven't figured out yet. Jesus is not impressed. He orders them to leave and allows them to choose their way of escape. He doesn't say anything to the man himself until the demons are gone. This is not a cure; it is an exorcism.

Why would Jesus send some poor farmer's entire herd over the cliff? Some Scripture scholars suggest that the pig story is not a news report but rather a metaphorical explanation of what just happened. Jews consider pigs to be ritually unclean and unfit for human consumption. Since nothing unclean is permitted in the kingdom, how appropriate for unclean spirits to ride a stampeding herd of unclean animals to destruction. Anyway, to Jewish storytellers, pigs—on a level with rats and cockroaches in their estimation—were not the point. What the demons did to the pigs, they would cheerfully have done to people. Two thousand pigs are worth nothing compared to one dirty, naked, homeless, insane, dangerous human being.

Mark 5:14–20. The noise of two thousand squealing pigs with eight thousand hooves pounding toward the cliff and dropping into the sea would have attracted a crowd even if the swineherds hadn't run to tell the story. No wonder people want Jesus out of there. If this man can provoke an avalanche of pigs, what else might he do? The healed man, though, knows that the pig riot was entirely for his benefit, and he wants to sign up as a disciple. For once, Jesus does not ask people to be quiet. Instead, he tells the man to talk. We hear a lot about "marginalized" people today. This man isn't even near the margins—he is as far from civilized society as a human being can get. And he becomes the first apostle—that is, one sent on a mission—to the gentiles.

Questions for Application

40 minutes
Choose questions according to your interest and time.

---

1 Read Isaiah 58:6–7 again. How are these needs handled in our society today? What is the role of churches in meeting these needs? What part does your parish play?

---

2 The man from the tombs lives completely outside society. Who are today's outcasts? Does your parish reach out to these people? Can you or your small group do something to help?

---

3 Is anyone ever too far gone for God to touch and heal and restore?

4 The people seem more afraid of Jesus than they are of the demon-possessed man. Why? Which would scare you more: if Jesus or the demon-possessed man lived across the street from your house? Why?

5 When the demons leave town, the pig industry suffers. Apparently, one man's livelihood went over the cliff in order to save another man's soul. Is this fair? Are similar sacrifices ever necessary today?

6 Why does Jesus want this man to talk about him? Does he want you to talk? What mercy has he shown you? Who needs to know?

In the sacred books it is the heavenly Father Himself who meets His children with tender love and enters into conversation with them.

The Pope and bishops of the Catholic Church at Vatican Council II (1965), *Dogmatic Constitution on Divine Revelation*

Approach to Prayer

15 minutes
Use one or both of these approaches—or create your own!

◆ Divide into two groups, A and B, and read alternating lines from Psalm 146:5–10.

A Happy are those whose help is the God of Jacob,
B whose hope is in the LORD their God,
A who made heaven and earth,
B the sea, and all that is in them;
A who keeps faith forever;
B who executes justice for the oppressed;
who gives food to the hungry.

A The LORD sets the prisoners free;
B the LORD opens the eyes of the blind.
A The LORD lifts up those who are bowed down;
B the LORD loves the righteous. . . .

A The LORD will reign forever,
B your God, O Zion, for all generations.
A and B Praise the LORD!

◆ Continue praying for loved ones and sharing results.

A Living Tradition

Exorcism

This section is a supplement for individual reading.

Jesus was an exorcist. He healed the sick *and* cast out demons. He gave the twelve disciples "authority over the unclean spirits," and they, too, "cast out many demons" as part of their healing work (see Mark 6:7–13). By the third century AD, exorcist was one of the Church's minor orders, and until 1983 each diocese was required to have its own exorcist. The Rite of Christian Initiation of Adults provides for "minor exorcisms"—prayers that the catechumens will be protected from evil.

The Church treats major exorcism very carefully. Some problems that appear to be demon possession are actually illnesses. In other situations, a person suffers from the results of evil but is not actually possessed by an evil spirit. There is no point trying to exorcize a demon when the cause of the trouble is something else. Sometimes, however, a demon does attack an individual, and nobody who has seen the malevolent power of genuine demon possession takes exorcism lightly. The *Catechism of the Catholic Church* (section 1673) highlights the need to proceed with extreme caution when demon possession is suspected, paying close attention to the Church's regulations:

When the Church asks publicly and authoritatively in the name of Jesus Christ that a person or object be protected against the power of the Evil One and withdrawn from his dominion, it is called *exorcism*. Jesus performed exorcisms and from him the Church has received the power and office of exorcizing.[1] In a simple form, exorcism is performed at the celebration of Baptism. The solemn exorcism, called "a major exorcism," can be performed only by a priest and with the permission of the bishop. The priest must proceed with prudence, strictly observing the rules established by the Church. Exorcism is directed at the expulsion of demons or to the liberation from demonic possession through the spiritual authority which Jesus entrusted to his Church. Illness, especially psychological illness, is a very different matter; treating this is the concern of medical science. Therefore, before an exorcism is performed, it is important to ascertain that one is dealing with the presence of the Evil One, and not an illness.[2]

[1] Cf. *Mk* 1:25–26; 3:15; 6:7, 13; 16:17.
[2] Cf. *Codex Iuris Canonici*, Can. 1172.

Amazing Grace

Questions to Begin

15 minutes
Use a question or two to get warmed up for the reading.

1 When you were little, were you afraid of the dark? What did you think lurked there?

2 Someone offers you a hundred dollars to jump fully clothed into a public swimming pool. What do you do? What if the person is your boss? your pastor? your best friend? a police officer? a total stranger? Mel Gibson?

Opening the Bible

5 minutes
*Read the passage aloud. Let individuals take turns reading
sections.*

The Reading: Isaiah 60:1–3; John 9:1–25, 31–38

Your Light Has Come

Isaiah 60:1 Arise, shine; for your light has come,
and the glory of the LORD has risen upon you.
2 For darkness shall cover the earth,
and thick darkness the peoples;
but the LORD will arise upon you,
and his glory will appear over you.
3 Nations shall come to your light,
and kings to the brightness of your dawn.

Who Sinned?

John 9:1 As he walked along, he saw a man blind from birth. 2 His
disciples asked him, "Rabbi, who sinned, this man or his parents, that
he was born blind?" 3 Jesus answered, "Neither this man nor his
parents sinned; he was born blind so that God's works might be
revealed in him. . . . 6 When he had said this, he spat on the ground
and made mud with the saliva and spread the mud on the man's eyes,
7 saying to him, "Go, wash in the pool of Siloam" (which means
Sent). Then he went and washed and came back able to see.

8 The neighbors and those who had seen him before as a
beggar began to ask, "Is this not the man who used to sit and beg?"
9 Some were saying, "It is he." Others were saying, "No, but it is
someone like him." He kept saying, "I am the man." 10 But they
kept asking him, "Then how were your eyes opened?" 11 He
answered, "The man called Jesus made mud, spread it on my eyes,
and said to me, "Go to Siloam and wash." Then I went and washed
and received my sight." 12 They said to him, "Where is he?" He
said, "I do not know."

The Religious Leaders Object

13 They brought to the Pharisees the man who had formerly been
blind. 14 Now it was a sabbath day when Jesus made the mud and
opened his eyes. 15 Then the Pharisees also began to ask him how he
had received his sight. He said to them, "He put mud on my eyes.
Then I washed, and now I see." 16 Some of the Pharisees said, "This

man is not from God, for he does not observe the sabbath." But others said, "How can a man who is a sinner perform such signs?" And they were divided. 17 So they said again to the blind man, "What do you say about him? It was your eyes he opened." He said, "He is a prophet."

18 The Jews* did not believe that he had been blind and had received his sight until they called the parents of the man who had received his sight 19 and asked them, "Is this your son, who you say was born blind? How then does he now see?" 20 His parents answered, "We know that this is our son, and that he was born blind; 21 but we do not know how it is that now he sees, nor do we know who opened his eyes. Ask him; he is of age. He will speak for himself." . . .

Seeing Is Believing

24 So for the second time they called the man who had been blind, and they said to him, "Give glory to God! We know that this man is a sinner." 25 He answered, "I do not know whether he is a sinner. One thing I do know, that though I was blind, now I see. . . . 31 We know that God does not listen to sinners, but he does listen to one who worships him and obeys his will. 32 Never since the world began has it been heard that anyone opened the eyes of a person born blind. 33 If this man were not from God, he could do nothing." 34 They answered him, "You were born entirely in sins, and are you trying to teach us?" And they drove him out.

35 Jesus heard that they had driven him out, and when he found him, he said, "Do you believe in the Son of Man?" 36 He answered, "And who is he, sir? Tell me, so that I may believe in him." 37 Jesus said to him, "You have seen him, and the one speaking with you is he." 38 He said, "Lord, I believe." And he worshiped him.

*In this case meaning the Pharisees.

10 minutes
Choose questions according to your interest and time.

1 In the Isaiah reading, where will the Lord's glory be seen? Who will see it? What will be the result?

2 Compare this healing to the healing of the blind man in Mark 8:22–26 (Week 2). What is different about the initial encounters of the men with Jesus? What is different about the healings themselves? Is John more interested in the miracle or in something else? What?

3 This healing incident involves a lot of discussion about sin. What are the disciples' concerns? the Pharisees'? How does Jesus respond to each group?

4 Why do the Pharisees think the blind man is a sinner? Why does Jesus think he is not? Why does the blind man disagree with the Pharisees as to whether Jesus is a sinner?

5 When does the man realize who Jesus is? Does he show any signs of belief before he is healed?

A Guide to the Reading

If participants have not read this section already, read it aloud. Otherwise go on to "Questions for Application."

The kingdom of God is breaking out all over, for those who can see by the light of Christ.

Isaiah 60:1–3. Some of the first words in John's Gospel are reminiscent of Isaiah's poem: "The light shines in the darkness, and the darkness did not overcome it" (John 1:5). In Isaiah, the "glory of the Lord" pierces through the earth's "thick darkness" and reveals God's people. Amazed, people from around the world—"nations" and "kings"—turn to see what God is doing.

John 9:1–12. It is early autumn. Jesus and his disciples have walked from Galilee to Jerusalem, a distance of some sixty miles, to observe the Festival of Booths. This thanksgiving festival, a commemoration of Israel's forty years in the wilderness, is also a joyous harvest celebration. Every morning a procession of priests carries water from the pool of Siloam to the temple to sprinkle on the altar. By night the temple is bathed in light from four giant torches, a light so intense it is said to illuminate every courtyard in the city. Light in the darkness, water of blessing—these are on people's minds when Jesus sees a blind beggar by the road.

Unlike many of the people Jesus heals, this man doesn't cry out. He doesn't try to grab Jesus' cloak. He doesn't kneel down and beg. He just sits there while the disciples carry on a philosophical discussion. Why is the world full of sickness, pain, and death? Are not these all the result of sin? Well then, whose sin? Do I suffer because I did something wrong, or because my parents or my ancestors or Adam and Eve went astray? Take this poor blind beggar, for instance. Is he blind because he's a sinner? Or, since he looks like he must have been blind from birth, was it something his parents did?

Jesus' answer is startling. "You're asking the wrong questions," he says. The cause of this man's blindness isn't the point. What's important is its *purpose.* This man's blindness provides an opportunity for God to reveal what he can do. Then Jesus mixes up a muddy paste, daubs it on the man's eyes, and sends him away to wash it off. So far the man hasn't said a word. But when he shows up again, now with 20/20 vision, he has to say something to his startled acquaintances. "It's me, all right," he assures them, "but how would I know where Jesus is? Remember, I've never even seen the guy!"

John 9:13–21. The Pharisees were an influential group who studied, debated, and carefully observed Jewish law. According to their way of thinking, Jesus never paid enough attention to traditional observances. When they hear about this healing, they are annoyed. First, Jesus has healed on a Sabbath day—a day when making clay and bathing are forbidden by the Pharisees' traditions. Jesus, they conclude, is a Sabbath breaker and therefore a sinner. However, a blind-from-birth beggar is running around town telling people Jesus has healed him, and his parents are backing up his story. What to do? The last thing Jerusalem needs is a law-breaking celebrity!

John 9:24–25, 31–38. The Pharisees try again and again to find flaws in the man's story, to no avail. The man can see, and he is convinced that his healer is from God. Eventually, the frustrated legal scholars drive the beggar away. And that's when Jesus comes looking for him, tells him he is the "Son of Man"—the one God has sent into the world to bring salvation—and accepts his worship.

Theologian René Latourelle describes four different responses to this miracle. Most of the onlookers are amazed but do not reflect on the miracle's meaning. They forget it entirely when something new captures their interest. Some, like the Pharisees, reflect on the miracle but do not believe. A few, like the man's parents, reflect and believe but stay quiet out of fear. One, the man himself, reflects, believes, and bears witness to Jesus.

In the end, these are the responses all of us must choose among whenever we see traces of God's kingdom. The glory of the Lord has risen upon us. The anointed one is at work in the world. Do we see? reflect? believe? bear witness?

Questions for Application

40 minutes
Choose questions according to your interest and time.

1 Think of a time when you felt suddenly illuminated (either literally or metaphorically). What brought you out of darkness?

2 How does the story about the man born blind influence your beliefs on the relationship between sin and illness? Is illness a punishment? Is healing a reward for being good?

3 The Pharisees are blind to some things that the formerly blind man sees clearly. What do the Pharisees not understand? Why is their vision obscured? What can stand in the way of our understanding?

4 Why do the parents answer evasively? (See John 9:22–23 for John's interpretation.) Do you ever hesitate to let your faith be known? Why?

5 How are God's works revealed in the blind man? Could God's works have been revealed in him if he had not been healed? How are God's works revealed in you?

6 What have you learned from these six weeks with the Bible about the kingdom of God?

7 What have you learned about Jesus' healing care for you?

Offer prayer with the expectation that God, through His Holy Spirit, may want to relieve the suffering, restore the person's health, rebuild the broken and bruised places, and bring glory to Himself by sovereignly intervening on the person's behalf, in the context of your group.

Thom Corrigan, *101 Great Ideas to Create a Caring Group*

Approach to Prayer

15 minutes
Use one or both of these approaches—or create your own!

◆ Pray together these words attributed to the third-century theologian Origen of Alexandria:

May the Lord Jesus touch our
    eyes,
as he did those of the blind.
Then we shall begin to see in
    visible things
those which are invisible.
May he open our eyes to gaze,
    not on present realities,
but on blessings to come.
May he open the eyes of our
    heart
to contemplate God in Spirit,
through Christ Jesus the Lord, to
    whom belongs
power and glory through all
    eternity.

◆ Share with one another your answered prayers and continuing concerns. You may wish to agree to continue praying together in coming weeks. Conclude by joining hands, if you are comfortable doing so, and praying an Our Father and a Glory to the Father.

Saints in the Making

St. Pio of Pietrelcina

This section is a supplement for individual reading.

Despite scorching heat, St. Peter's Square was packed and overflowing. An estimated three hundred thousand people—one of the largest groups ever to assemble there—had gathered to see Pope John Paul II confer sainthood upon a Franciscan friar, Padre Pio. Only thirty-four years since his death at eighty-one, Padre Pio was beloved by millions worldwide.

Francesco Forgione was given the name Pio when he joined the Capuchin Franciscans at age fifteen. During the next sixty-five years, he became well-known as a healer. According to contemporary journalists, people with deformities from old injuries, polio, and rickets threw away their canes and braces and walked when he prayed for them. Kidney disease, tuberculosis, cancers, and even blindness succumbed to his healing touch. After his death in 1968, reports of cures through his intercession continued. Two of these were examined by the Vatican and declared genuine miracles: the 1995 healing of a woman with a ruptured thoracic duct, and the 2000 healing of a seven-year-old boy with meningitis.

Pope John Paul II called Padre Pio "a miraculous healer," but he warned that healing was not the most important element in the saint's life: "Padre Pio's witness is a powerful call to the supernatural dimension, not to be confused with exaggerated concern for miracles, a deviation which he always and resolutely shunned." More important were the saint's life of constant prayer, his love for the Eucharist, and his willingness to give spiritual direction and sacramental Reconciliation to a growing stream of penitents.

If Padre Pio followed Jesus Christ by healing people in body and in soul, he also followed him in suffering. For most of his life he, like St. Francis of Assisi, bore the stigmata—painful, supernaturally inflicted wounds in hands, feet, and side like Christ's wounds on the cross. He also lived with slander and outright persecution from some in authority who either were jealous of his large following or misunderstood the nature of his life and work. Nevertheless, he continued to obey his superiors and to do his assigned tasks, often describing himself as "a poor Franciscan who prays." His feast day is September 23.

Why Doesn't Jesus Heal Everybody?

If the kingdom of God began to break into human history some two thousand years ago, why are so many of us still sick? in pain? grieving for loved ones who have died? According to the Gospels, Jesus and his disciples would go through a town and cure everyone for miles around (see, for example, Matthew 9:35; Mark 6:56; and Luke 9:1–6). Why doesn't Jesus heal everybody now? How hard can it be?

A lot of people do believe God has healed them, of course. We've briefly looked at healings through a French shrine (p. 41), a priest in California (p. 51), and an Italian Franciscan (p. 71). Some people report improved health and even miraculous cures after receiving the sacrament of Anointing of the Sick (p. 74). And yet epidemics still rage, accidents still happen, and people still die. Why? Only God knows why some prayers for healing are answered and some, apparently, are not. Here are some thoughts that may help us find meaning in what we cannot understand.

Some people don't ask to be healed. Time and again, Jesus commends people for their faith—for example, the woman who has hemorrhaged for many years (Week 3), the military officer, and the Canaanite mother (Week 4). This faith is not a vague feeling of spirituality. It is the conviction that Jesus can heal, a belief strong enough to send the sick people or their loved ones to Jesus for help. For the most part, people who stay home miss out, though Jesus goes to a remote graveyard to release a demon-possessed man (Week 5). The blind beggar (Week 6), who does not ask to be healed, comes to faith after Jesus heals him anyway. God knows our faith is weak, and he makes allowances. But if we believe Jesus is able to heal the sick, it's a good idea to ask.

Some people ask, but God has other plans for them. Despite much prayer, Father Richard Bain (p. 51) still suffers from a debilitating hearing disorder; he believes his pain increases his empathy and helps him to be humble. Joni Eareckson Tada, a quadriplegic since a diving accident in 1967, was not healed as she once thought she would be; she has become one of America's leading advocates for the disabled. St. Paul had some ailment that he called his thorn in the flesh. He prayed three times that it would be taken away, to no avail. The Lord told him: "My grace is sufficient for you, for power is made perfect in weakness" (2 Corinthians 12:7–9). Sometimes God restores people to health; sometimes God gives people the grace and strength to live with their pain.

Some people ask for one kind of healing and receive another. When journalist Kimberly Winston began research for an article about people who had prayed for healing but were not healed, she expected to find a lot of angry, disillusioned atheists. To her surprise, most interviewees said their faith had increased in spite of ongoing illness. In *Faith Beyond Faith Healing,* Winston writes: "Virtually everyone had come to rethink their idea of what faith healing includes, moving from the belief that it could mean only a cure for their physical condition, to believing it could mean patching up relationships, overcoming addictions, and, most important, finding some peace." See the next article for a list of ways a person can be healed by the sacrament of Anointing, even when physical healing does not occur.

Someday everybody will be healed. The kingdom of God has already broken into our world, but it is not yet here in fullness. Not every disease is cured. All people—including those who have been miraculously healed—eventually die. We pray for the kingdom to come, for God's will to be "done on earth as it is in heaven." Every Sunday we say these words from the Nicene Creed: "He will come again in glory to judge the living and the dead, and his kingdom will have no end." We do not know when or how the kingdom will come in glory, so meanwhile we obey our Lord by waiting patiently and watching for signs of the kingdom in our midst. One day, we believe, God's kingdom will fill the earth. "The kingdom of the world" will become "the kingdom of our Lord and of his Messiah," and "mourning and crying and pain will be no more" (Revelation 11:15; 21:4). In that day every person will be healed, and all creation will become new.

The Healing Sacraments

The Catholic Church celebrates two sacraments of healing. Through the sacrament of Reconciliation, God heals the damage caused by sin. Through the sacrament of Anointing of the Sick, God heals the damage inflicted by illness, injury, and old age.

Jesus often associated forgiveness with healing. For example, he sent his disciples out to preach repentance and to heal diseases. The Gospel of Mark reports that they "went out and proclaimed that all should repent." They also "anointed with oil many who were sick and cured them" (6:12–13). The New Testament letter of James advises those who are sick to "call for the elders of the church and have them pray over them, anointing them with oil in the name of the Lord." If they do this, he says, "the prayer of faith will save the sick, and the Lord will raise them up; and anyone who has committed sins will be forgiven. Therefore confess your sins to one another, and pray for one another, so that you may be healed" (James 5:14–16).

The sacraments of healing followed a complex path of development through the early centuries of the Church. While Reconciliation (often called confession or Penance) became widely used, healing tended to be reserved for a person's final illness. In fact, the sacrament of Anointing of the Sick became known as Extreme Unction, "Final Anointing," as it was used primarily when a person received the "last rites" on his or her deathbed.

A shift in emphasis happened in the mid-twentieth century. The sacraments of healing, theologians said, are meant for the living just as much as for the dying. Anointing should continue to be offered to those at the point of death—but it should be available to other ill and injured Christians as well.

When can the sacrament of Anointing of the Sick be received? In 1963, a document of the Second Vatican Council, *The Constitution on the Sacred Liturgy* (section 73), recommended that the sacrament be offered more widely:

"Extreme Unction," which may also and more fittingly be called "Anointing of the Sick," is not a sacrament for those only who are at the point of death. Hence, as soon as any one of the faithful begins to be in danger of death from sickness or old age, the fitting time for him to receive this sacrament has certainly already arrived.

The *Catechism of the Catholic Church,* first published in 1994, teaches that Anointing of the Sick is for anyone who is "experiencing the difficulties inherent in the condition of grave illness or old age." No longer is it necessarily a one-time-only experience. "Each time a Christian falls seriously ill, he may receive the Anointing of the Sick, and also when, after he has received it, the illness worsens" (sections 1527, 1529).

What happens when Anointing of the Sick is celebrated? Though Catholics everywhere understand this sacrament in much the same way, the exact procedure followed differs from place to place. In the rite used by most American Catholics, Anointing of the Sick often happens during a celebration of the Mass. After the homily, prayers are offered for the sick and their caregivers. Sick people come to the altar, where the priest lays his hands on their heads and anoints them with oil, saying: "Through this holy anointing may the Lord in his love and mercy help you with the grace of the Holy Spirit. May the Lord who frees you from sin save you and raise you up" (*Catechism of the Catholic Church,* section 1513). After the Anointing, the Eucharist continues as usual.

If the sick person is homebound or bedridden, the priest leads a similar ritual in the presence of friends and family members. Holy Communion may be received after the Anointing.

Will Anointing restore the sick person's physical health? Yes, according to the Catechism (section 1532), "if it is conducive to the salvation of his soul." But physical healing is not its major purpose. The sacrament also

- ◆ unites "the sick person to the passion of Christ, for his own good and that of the whole Church"
- ◆ gives the person strength, "peace, and courage to endure in a Christian manner the sufferings of illness or old age"
- ◆ offers "forgiveness of sins, if the sick person was not able to obtain it through the sacrament of Penance"
- ◆ prepares the person to pass "over to eternal life."

Both Anointing and Reconciliation are truly sacraments of healing—actions by which God restores wholeness to body, mind, and soul.

Suggestions for Bible Discussion Groups

Like a camping trip, a Bible discussion group works best if you agree on where you're going and how you intend to get there. Many groups use their first meeting to talk over such questions and reach a consensus. Here is a checklist of issues, with bits of advice from people who have experience in Bible discussions. (A planning discussion will go more smoothly if the leaders have thought through the following issues beforehand.)

Agree on your purpose. Are you getting together to gain wisdom and direction for your lives? to finally get acquainted with the Bible? to support one another in following Christ? to encourage those who are exploring—or reexploring—the Church? for other reasons?

Agree on attitudes. For example: "We're all beginners here." "We're here to help one another understand and respond to God's word." "We're not here to offer counseling or direction to one another." "We want to read Scripture prayerfully." What do *you* wish to emphasize? Make it explicit!

Agree on ground rules. Barbara J. Fleischer, in her useful book *Facilitating for Growth,* recommends that a group clearly state its approach to the following:

- *Preparation.* Do we agree to read the material and prepare answers to the questions before each meeting?
- *Attendance.* What kind of priority will we give to our meetings?
- *Self-revelation.* Are we willing to help the others in the group gradually get to know us—our weaknesses as well as our strengths, our needs as well as our gifts?
- *Listening.* Will we commit ourselves to listening to one another?
- *Confidentiality.* Will we keep everything that is shared *with* the group *in* the group?
- *Discretion.* Will we refrain from sharing about the faults and sins of people who are not in the group?
- *Encouragement and support.* Will we give as well as receive?
- *Participation.* Will we give each person the time and opportunity to make a contribution?

You could probably take a pen and draw a circle around *listening* and *confidentiality*. Those two points are especially important.

The following items could be added to Fleischer's list:

- *Relationship with parish.* Is our group part of the adult faith-formation program? independent but operating with the express approval of the pastor? not a parish-based group?
- *New members.* Will we let new members join us once we have begun the six weeks of discussions?

Agree on housekeeping.

- *When will we meet?*
- *How often will we meet?* Meeting weekly or every other week is best if you can manage it. William Riley remarks, "Meetings once a month are too distant from each other for the threads of the last session not to be lost" *(The Bible Study Group: An Owner's Manual).*
- *How long will each meeting run?*
- *Where will we meet?*
- *Is any setup needed?* Christine Dodd writes that "the problem with meeting in a place like a church hall is that it can be very soul-destroying," given the cold, impersonal feel of many church facilities. If you have to meet in a church facility, Dodd recommends doing something to make the area homey *(Making Scripture Work).*
- *Who will host the meetings?* Leaders and hosts are not necessarily the same people.
- *Will we have refreshments?* Who will provide them? Don Cousins and Judson Poling make this recommendation: "Serve refreshments if you like, but save snacks and other foods for the end of the meeting to minimize distractions" *(Leader's Guide 1).*
- *What about child care?* Most experienced leaders of Bible discussion groups discourage bringing infants or other children to adult Bible discussions.

Agree on leadership. You need someone to facilitate—to keep the discussion on track, to see that everyone has a chance to speak, to help the group stay on schedule. Rena Duff, editor of the newsletter *Sharing God's Word Today,* recommends having two or three people take turns leading the discussions.

It's okay if the leader is not an expert on the Bible. You have this Six Weeks book as a guide, and if questions come up that no one can answer, you can delegate a participant to do a little research between meetings. Perhaps someone on the pastoral staff of your parish could offer advice. Or help may be available from your diocesan catechetical office or a local Catholic college or seminary.

It's important for the leader to set an example of listening, to draw out the quieter members (and occasionally restrain the more vocal ones), to move the group on when it gets stuck, to remind the members of their agreements, and to summarize what the group is accomplishing.

Bible discussion is an opportunity to experience the fulfillment of Jesus' promise "Where two or three are gathered in my name, I am there among them" (Matthew 18:20). Put your discussion group in Jesus' hands. Pray for the guidance of the Spirit. And have a great time exploring God's word together!

Y ou can use this booklet just as well for individual study as for group discussion. While discussing the Bible with other people can be a rich experience, there are advantages to reading on your own. For example:

◆ You can focus on the points that interest you most.

◆ You can go at your own pace.

◆ You can be completely relaxed and unashamedly honest in your answers to all the questions, since you don't have to share them with anyone!

My suggestions for using this booklet on your own are these:

◆ Don't skip the Questions to Begin. The questions can help you as an individual reader warm up to the topic of the reading.

◆ Take your time on the Questions for Careful Reading and Questions for Application. While a group will probably not have enough time to work on all the questions, you can allow yourself the time to consider all of them if you are using the booklet by yourself.

◆ After reading the Guide to the Reading, go back and reread the Scripture text before answering the Questions for Application.

◆ Take the time to look up all the parenthetical Scripture references in the introduction, the Guides to the Readings, and the other material.

◆ Read additional sections of Scripture related to the excerpts in this book. For example, read the portions of Scripture that come before and after the sections that form the readings in this Six Weeks book. You will understand the readings better by viewing them in context in the Bible.

◆ Since you control the pace, give yourself plenty of opportunities to reflect on the meaning of Jesus' healing miracles for you. Let your reading be an opportunity for these words to become God's words to you.

Bibles

The following editions of the Bible contain the full set of biblical books recognized by the Catholic Church, along with a great deal of useful explanatory material:

◆ The Catholic Study Bible (Oxford University Press), which uses the text of the New American Bible

◆ The Catholic Bible: Personal Study Edition (Oxford University Press), which also uses the text of the New American Bible

◆ The New Jerusalem Bible, the regular (not the reader's) edition (Doubleday)

Books, Web Sites, and Other Resources

◆ Lyn Holley Doucet, *A Healing Walk with St. Ignatius: Discovering God's Presence in Difficult Times* (Chicago: Loyola Press, 2002).

◆ John P. Meier, *A Marginal Jew: Rethinking the Historical Jesus,* vol. 2, *Mentor, Message, and Miracles* (New York: Doubleday, 1994).

◆ Kimberly Winston, *Faith Beyond Faith Healing: Finding Hope after Shattered Dreams* (Brewster, MA: Paraclete Press, 2002).

◆ The full text of the *Catechism of the Catholic Church* is available online at http://www.usccb.org/catechism/.

How has Scripture had an impact on your life? Was this booklet helpful to you in your study of the Bible? Please send comments, suggestions, and personal experiences to Kevin Perrotta, General Editor, Trade Editorial Department, Loyola Press, 3441 N. Ashland Ave., Chicago, IL 60657.